curious about
LEPRECHAUNS

BY GINA KAMMER

What are you

curious about?

Curious About is published by Amicus
P.O. Box 227
Mankato, MN 56002
www.amicuspublishing.us

Editor: Alissa Thielges and Rebecca Glaser
Series Designer: Kathleen Petelinsek
Cover Designer: Catherine Berthiaume
Book Designer: Kathleen Petelinsek
Photo Researchers: Bridget Prehn and Omay Ayres

Library of Congress Cataloging-in-Publication Data
Names: Kammer, Gina, author.
Title: Curious about leprechauns / by Gina Kammer.
Description: Mankato, MN : Amicus, 2023. | Series: Curious
about mythical creatures | Includes bibliographical references
and index. | Audience: Ages 6–9 | Audience: Grades 2–3 |
Summary: "Survey the legends and folklore about leprechaun
appearance, behavior, and homes in a fun question-and-answer
format that reinforces inquiry-based learning for early elementary-
age readers. A Stay Curious! Learn More feature models research
skills and doubles as a mini media literacy lesson. Includes simple
infographics, glossary, and index"– Provided by publisher.
Identifiers: LCCN 2020001125 (print) | LCCN 2020001126
(ebook) | ISBN 9781645491286 (library binding) | ISBN
9781681526959 (paperback) | ISBN 9781645491705 (pdf)
Subjects: LCSH: Leprechauns–Juvenile literature.
| Folklore–Ireland–Juvenile literature.
Classification: LCC GR153.5 .K36 2021 (print) | LCC
GR153.5 (ebook) | DDC 398.209417–dc23
LC record available at https://lccn.loc.gov/2020001125
LC ebook record available at https://lccn.loc.gov/2020001126

Photos © Dreamstime / Linda Bucklin Cover, 1; Shutterstock /
mythja 2, 6–7; Dreamstime / Julien Tromeur 2, 6–7; Dreamstime
/ Linda Bucklin 4; Alamy / Peter Cavanagh 5; Shutterstock /
Susanitah 9; Shutterstock / Saibarakova Ilona 9; Dreamstime /
Alexey Konkov 9; Graft Studio / Murka 9; Wikimedia Commons
/ Tony DiTerlizzi 10; Shutterstock / ArtSvetlana 11; Dreamstime
/ Julien Tromeur 11; Shutterstock / VarnaK 12–13; Dreamstime /
Linda Bucklin 13; Creatures of Irish Folklore / Butte Broadcasting
Inc 15; Kathleen Petelinksek / Kathleen Petelinksek 16; Shutterstock
/ Lukiyanova Natalia frenta 16; Shutterstock / Jan Stria 17;
Dreamstime / Linda Bucklin 17; The Wallpapers / Unknown
18–19; Shutterstock / Pierdus 20–21; Shutterstock / Shyshell
22–23Dreamstime / Linda Bucklin Cover, 1; Shutterstock / mythja
2, 6–7; Dreamstime / Julien Tromeur 2, 6–7; Dreamstime / Linda
Bucklin 4; Alamy / Peter Cavanagh 5; Shutterstock / Susanitah 9;
Shutterstock / Saibarakova Ilona 9; Dreamstime / Alexey Konkov
9; Graft Studio / Murka 9; Wikimedia Commons / Tony DiTerlizzi
10; Shutterstock / ArtSvetlana 11; Dreamstime / Julien Tromeur
11; Shutterstock / VarnaK 12–13; Dreamstime / Linda Bucklin 13;
Creatures of Irish Folklore / Butte Broadcasting Inc 15; Kathleen
Petelinksek / Kathleen Petelinksek 16; Shutterstock / Lukiyanova
Natalia frenta 16; Shutterstock / Jan Stria 17; Dreamstime / Linda
Bucklin 17; The Wallpapers / Unknown 18–19; Shutterstock /
Pierdus 20–21; Shutterstock / Shyshell 22–23

CHAPTER THREE

Finding Leprechauns
PAGE
16

Are leprechauns real?

Stories about leprechauns go back 1,000 years. Leprechauns are a type of **fairy**. Some people think fairies were once rulers of Ireland. They believe that leprechauns still live there. But no one has **proof** they exist.

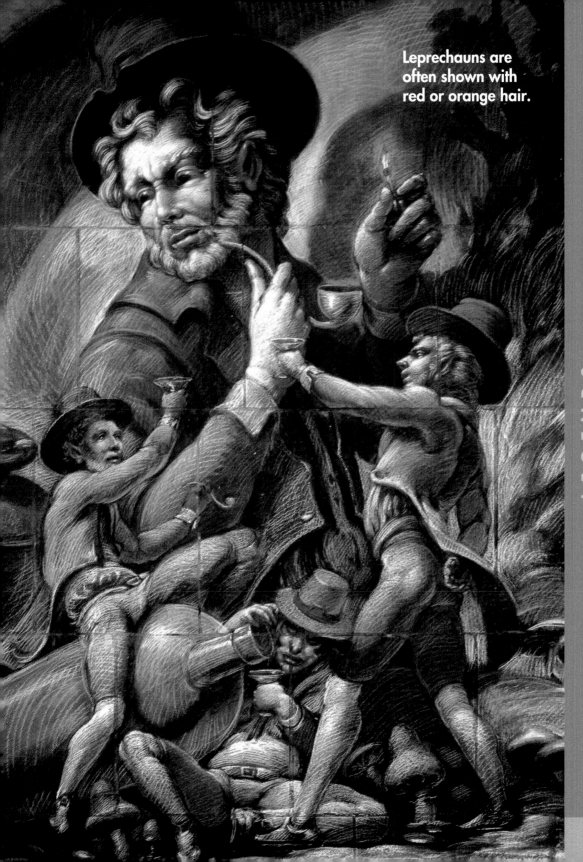

Leprechauns are often shown with red or orange hair.

What do leprechauns look like?

Many pictures show leprechauns with buckles on their hats and shoes.

In most stories, leprechauns are small men. They are about 2 feet (0.6 m) tall. They have wrinkled faces with red cheeks. Usually, leprechauns have beards. They wear red or green coats and hats. In older stories, leprechauns could be women, too.

COMPARING SIZES

How tall is a leprechaun?

leprechaun –
2 feet (0.6 m)

adult human –
6 feet (1.8 m)

What magic powers do leprechauns have?

Leprechauns are full of magic. They use it mostly to play tricks on people. They cheat at a magical game of hide-and-seek. They can appear anywhere and disappear in a blink. They even have the power to grant wishes!

Leprechauns often use their magical powers for mischief.

CHAPTER TWO

What do leprechauns like to do?

Leprechauns and other fairies love to play. They dance and play music. But leprechauns work hard, too. They make shoes, using tiny hammers. They are known for wearing nice shoes.

Stories say leprechauns are happy to work on shoes.

Do leprechauns really have pots of gold?

Rainbows form when the sun comes out after rain showers.

Leprechauns are rich. Maybe they make a lot of money from all their shoes! Or they might be **bankers** for fairies. However they got it, they don't want to share it. **Legends** say a leprechaun buries his pot of gold at the end of a rainbow

Are leprechauns friendly?

A leprechaun's pot of gold could make a person rich.

Leprechauns don't usually hurt people. People are always trying to catch them! Legends say leprechauns will give up their gold to get away. Or they might give you three wishes. But leprechauns are tricky. They really like to make **greedy** people look **foolish**.

Artists often show leprechauns with four-leaf clovers. Some people believe finding a four-leaf clover is good luck.

Where do leprechauns live?

Leprechauns live in Ireland. They like the countryside. They live alone, in homes hidden under the ground. Listen for tapping. That could be a leprechaun making a shoe with a hammer!

REPORTED LEPRECHAUN SIGHTINGS IN IRELAND

NORTHERN IRELAND •Belfast

IRELAND

Dublin ★

•Limerick

•Cork

■ More leprechaun sightings
■ Fewer leprechaun sightings

Fewer people live
in the countryside
than in towns.
Leprechauns can
stay hidden.

Has anyone seen a leprechaun?

HOW MANY LEPRECHAUNS ARE IN CARLINGFORD?

A man from Carlingford said a leprechaun told him there were only 236 of them left. The area is now protected, and leprechauns are included as one of the area's protected "species."

In old stories, greedy people did. There are new stories, too. In Carlingford, Ireland, a man found a leprechaun suit and coins. Since then, the town has a leprechaun hunt each year. But no one has found real leprechauns yet.

Leprechauns might make their homes in Ireland's rolling hills.

How could you find a leprechaun?

The hole in this tree would make a great leprechaun home.

Leprechauns hide well. Look hard for the doors to their homes. The openings might look like a rabbit's **burrow**. Or it might be a hole in a tree. If you spot a leprechaun, he can't leave while you watch. Don't blink! If you do, the leprechaun will disappear.

ASK MORE QUESTIONS

Where is the best place to look for leprechauns?

Do leprechauns wear the same clothes all the time?

Try a BIG QUESTION: Why do people search for leprechauns?

SEARCH FOR ANSWERS

Search the library catalog or the Internet.
A librarian, teacher, or parent can help you.

Using Keywords
Find the looking glass

Keywords are the most important words in your question.

?

If you want to know about:
- where to find leprechauns, type: WHERE LEPRECHAUNS LIVE
- what leprechauns wear in the legends, type: LEPRECHAUN CLOTHES LEGENDS

FIND GOOD SOURCES

Are the sources reliable?
Some sources are better than others. An adult can help you. Here are some good, safe sources.

Books
Curious about Fairies
by Gina Kammer, 2023.

Magic & Myth: Ireland's Fairy Tales
by Michael Scott, 2021.

Internet Sites
CBC Kids: The Legend of the Leprechaun
*https://www.cbc.ca/kidscbc2/
the-feed/the-legend-of-the-leprechaun*
CBC is public television in Canada. It has news and information on many topics.

National Leprechaun Museum
http://www.leprechaunmuseum.ie/mythicalforest/
The National Leprechaun Museum is in Ireland. Museums are good sources of research.
*Tip: click the button in the top left corner for other seasons.

Every effort has been made to ensure that these websites are appropriate for children. However, because of the nature of the Internet, it is impossible to guarantee that these sites will remain active indefinitely or that their contents will not be altered.

SHARE AND TAKE ACTION

Set up a leprechaun camera.
With the help of an adult, find a hole or burrow in the ground. Point the camera at the hole. Wait a day or two and see if you catch a leprechaun on camera!

Take a cave tour.
Find out what other things live under the ground. They might be neighbors with a leprechaun!

Ask an adult or librarian to help you learn about rainbows.
Then write down and share what you think. Could a pot of gold be buried at the end of a rainbow? Or would it have to be hidden with magic?

GLOSSARY

banker A person who works in a bank; banks lend or take care of money.

burrow A hole or tunnel in the ground that an animal makes to live in.

fairies Magical beings that often look like small people.

foolish Silly or not smart.

greedy Selfishly wanting more; eager to have something.

legend A story from the past that may or may not be true but cannot be checked.

proof Evidence of something.

INDEX

About the Author

Gina Kammer grew up writing and illustrating her own stories. Now she edits children's books and writes for all ages. She likes to read fantasy and medieval literature. She also enjoys traveling, oil painting, archery, and snuggling her grumpy bunny. She lives in Minnesota.